100 pictures

of zoo animals

100 Pictures of Zoo Animals
1st edition

Editor:Jonas Egebart
Text: Lianne Picot
Photos: PhotoArtel
Designer: Daniil Alexandrov

http://100thingsapp.com

This book is also available as app.
Search for "100 Zoo Animals" on App Store.

100 pictures
of zoo animals

TABLE OF

CONTENTS

Giant Anteater

Giant Anteaters have no teeth

Agouti

Agoutis live in Central and South America

Antelope

A group of Antelopes is called a herd

Llama

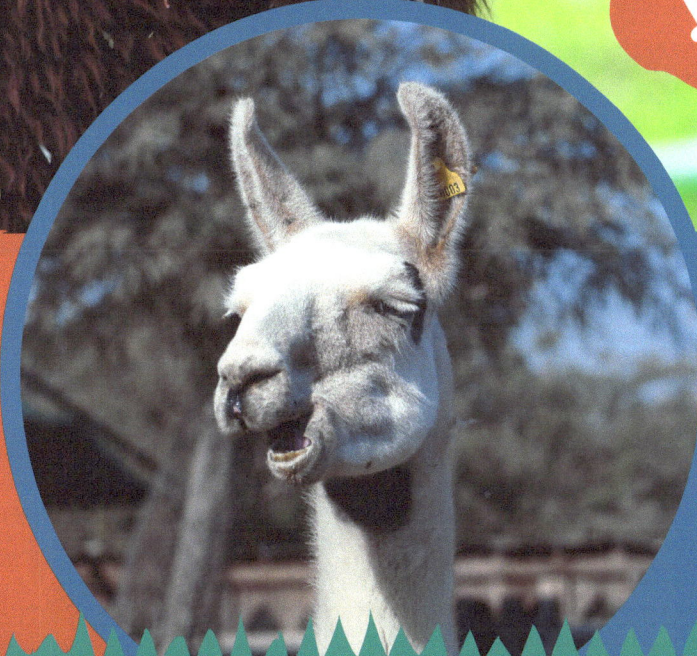

Lama groups are called herds

Lamas are very intelligent

Black Bear

Black Bears love to eat berries

Brown Bear

Brown Bears like to fish for salmon

The Black
Crowned Crane
is the only
crane that
nests in trees

Cardinal

Cardinals stay home in the winter

Capra

Capras live in the mountains

Camel

The Camel can run very fast

Cheetah

The Cheetah is the fastest animal on earth

Jaguar

Jaguars love swimming

White
Nosed Coati

White Nosed
Coatis love
to play fight

Chipmunk

Chipmunks store food in their cheeks

Chameleon

Chameleons change colours

Iguana

Iguanas lay eggs

Komodo Dragon

Komodo Dragons have lived on earth for millions of years

Jamaican Crocodile

Crocodiles love sunbathing

The Crocodile is the largest reptile

Cayman

Caymans live in hot places near lakes and rivers

Elephant

Wild Elephants live for up to 60 years

Elephants use their trunks for breathing, smelling and grabbing things!

24

Elephants really love their kids

A Baby Elephant is called a calf

Frog

Frog babies are called tadpoles

Salamander

Salamanders love hide and seek

Yellow Python

Yellow Pythons
make their homes
in caves and trees

Fox

Foxes are very clever

Wolf

Wolves live in packs

King Vulture dads look after the nest too

King
Vulture

Gyps

Gyps live in Asia

Giraffes sleep standing up

Giraffe

Rhino

Rhinoceros means "nose horn"

The Giraffe and the Rhino live together in Africa

Gorilla

Gorillas live in groups called troops

Gorillas walk on their knuckles

Orangutan

Orangutans sleep in nests

Orangutans make their own tools to help find food

Hippopotamus

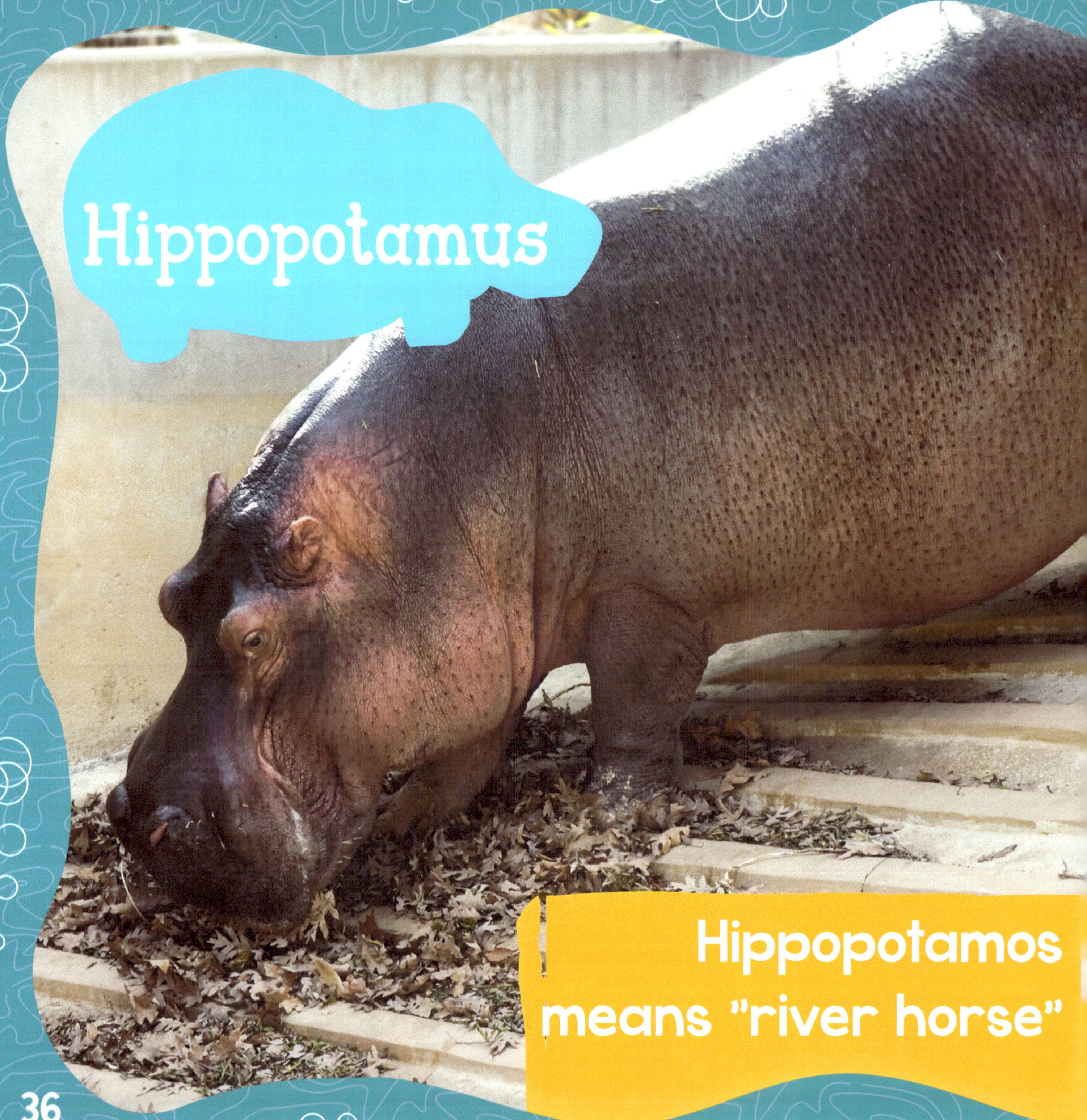

Hippopotamos means "river horse"

Hippos live in Africa

Hippos love the water

Golden Jackal

The Jackal is part of the dog family

Hyena

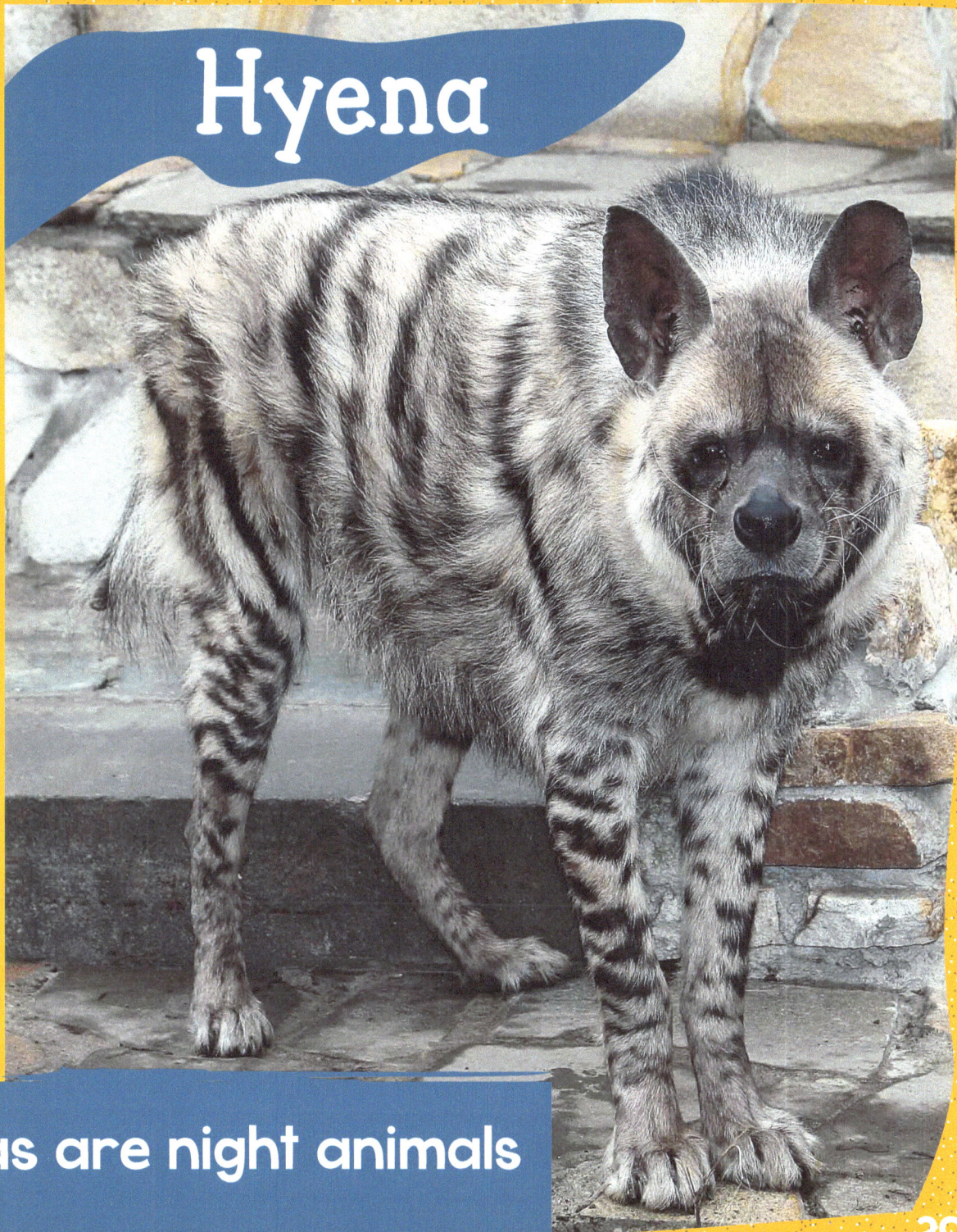

Hyenas are night animals

Lemur

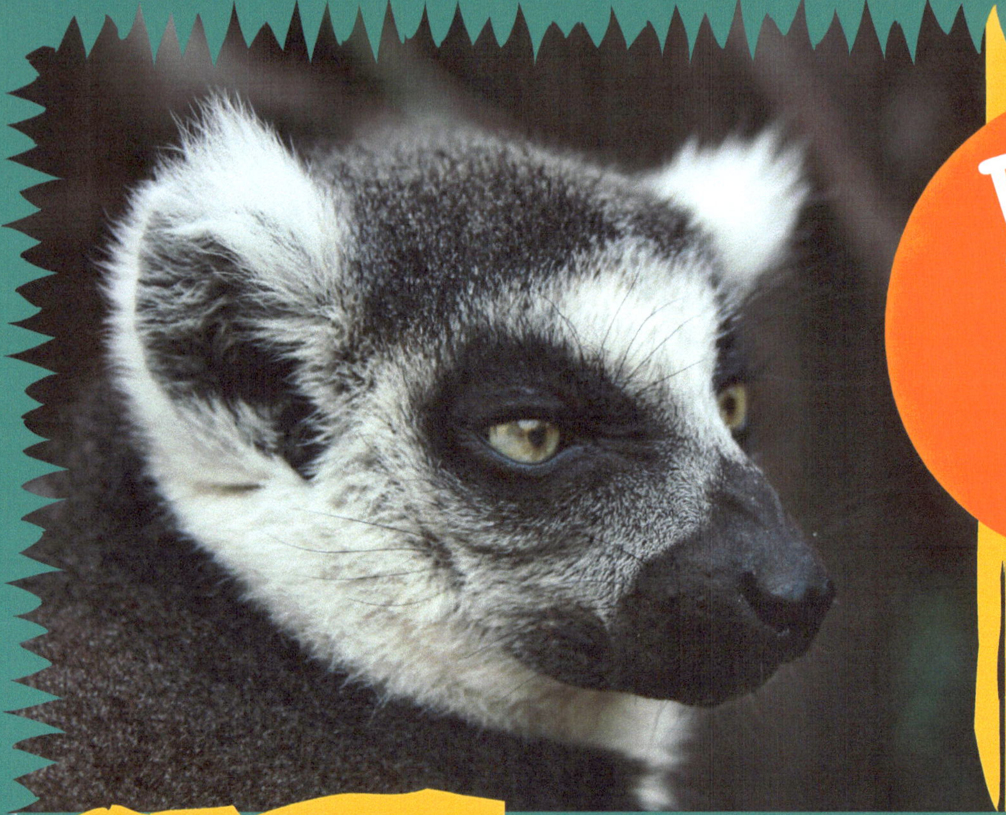

Lemurs come from Madagascar

Lemurs love to eat fruit

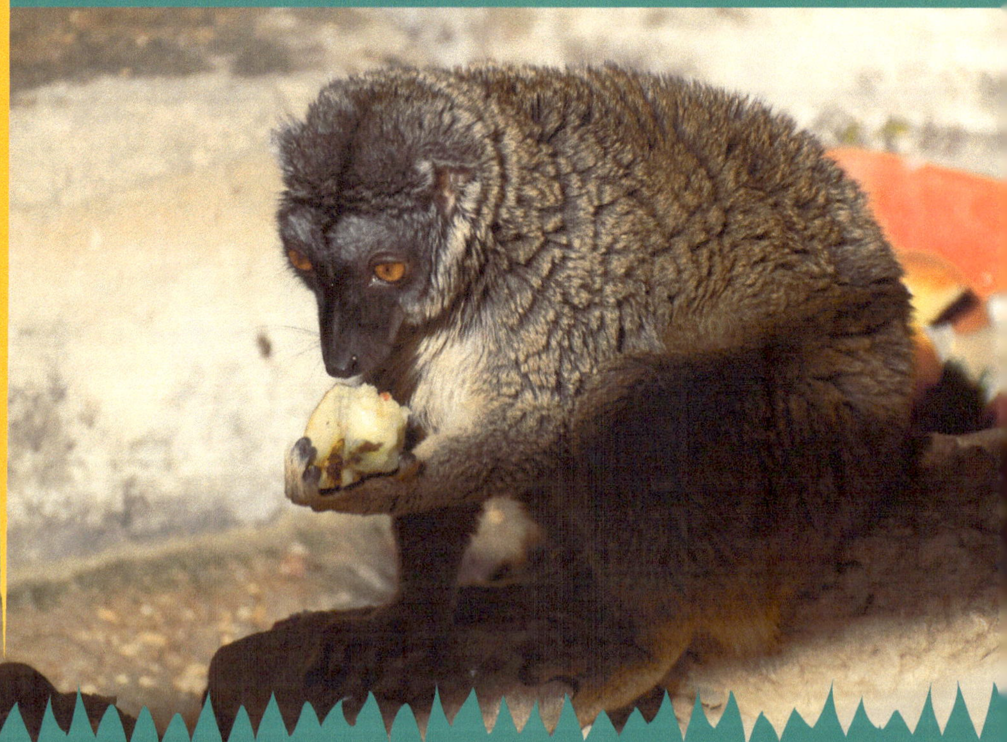

Raccoon

Raccoons sleep in trees

Leopard

The Leopard is the smallest of the big cats

Leopards love climbing trees

42

Lynx

The Lynx looks like he has a beard!

Lions can weigh
up to 550 pounds

Lion

This Lion is
from Africa

The Lioness looks after the cubs

The Lioness is in charge of the hunting

White Face
Saki Monkey

Saki Monkeys
love to eat
berries

Saki Monkeys sleep like cats on branches

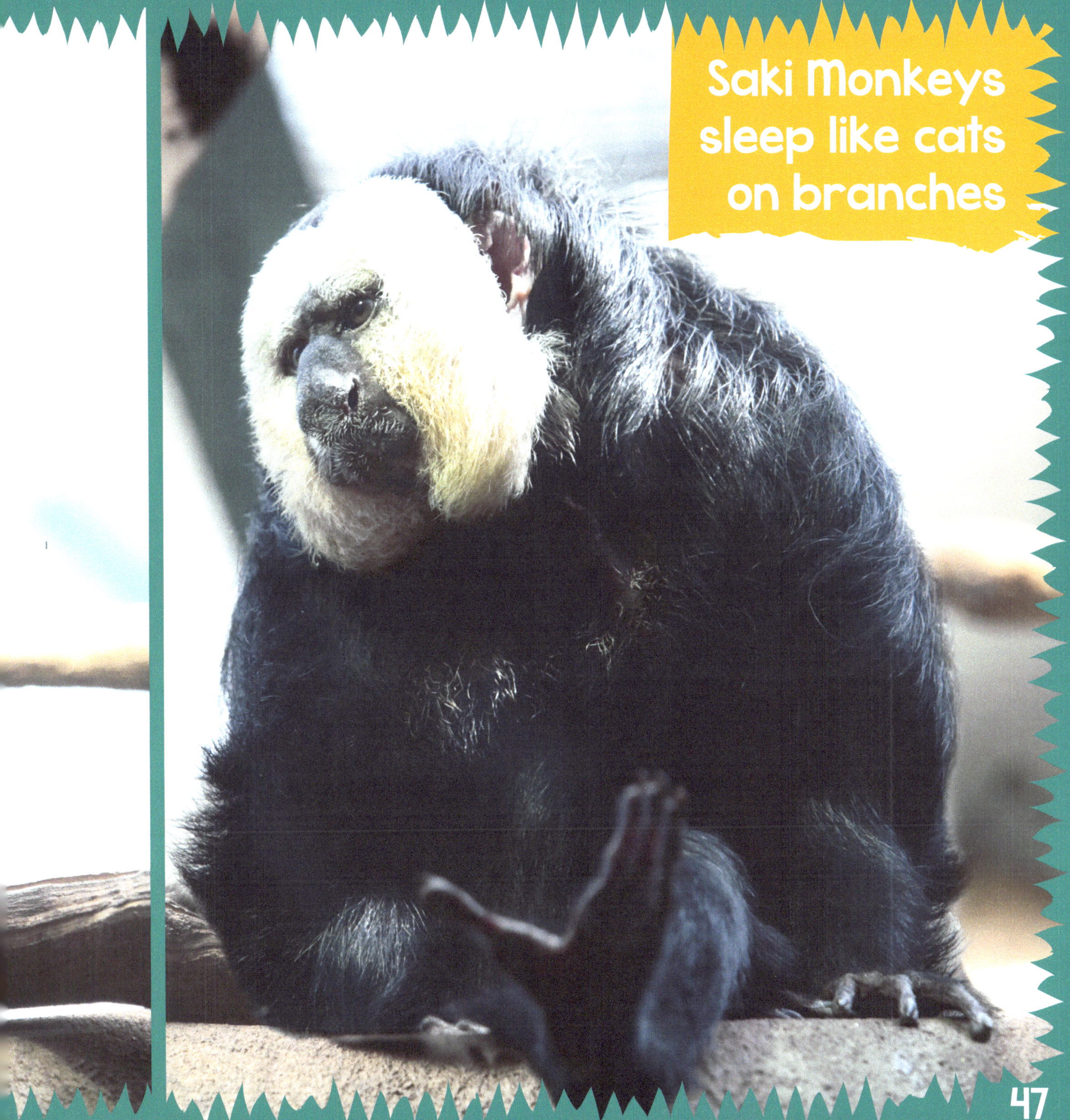

Macaque

The Macaque monkey is from Japan

Monkey

Monkeys are full of mischief!

Monkeys like to eat leaves

Yellow Baboon

Yellow Baboons
live in troops

Mandril

Mandril monkeys are the largest monkeys

Opossum

Opossums play dead when they are scared

52

Sloth Bear

Sloth Bears like to climb trees

Sloth Bears eat termites and fruit

53

Asian Otter

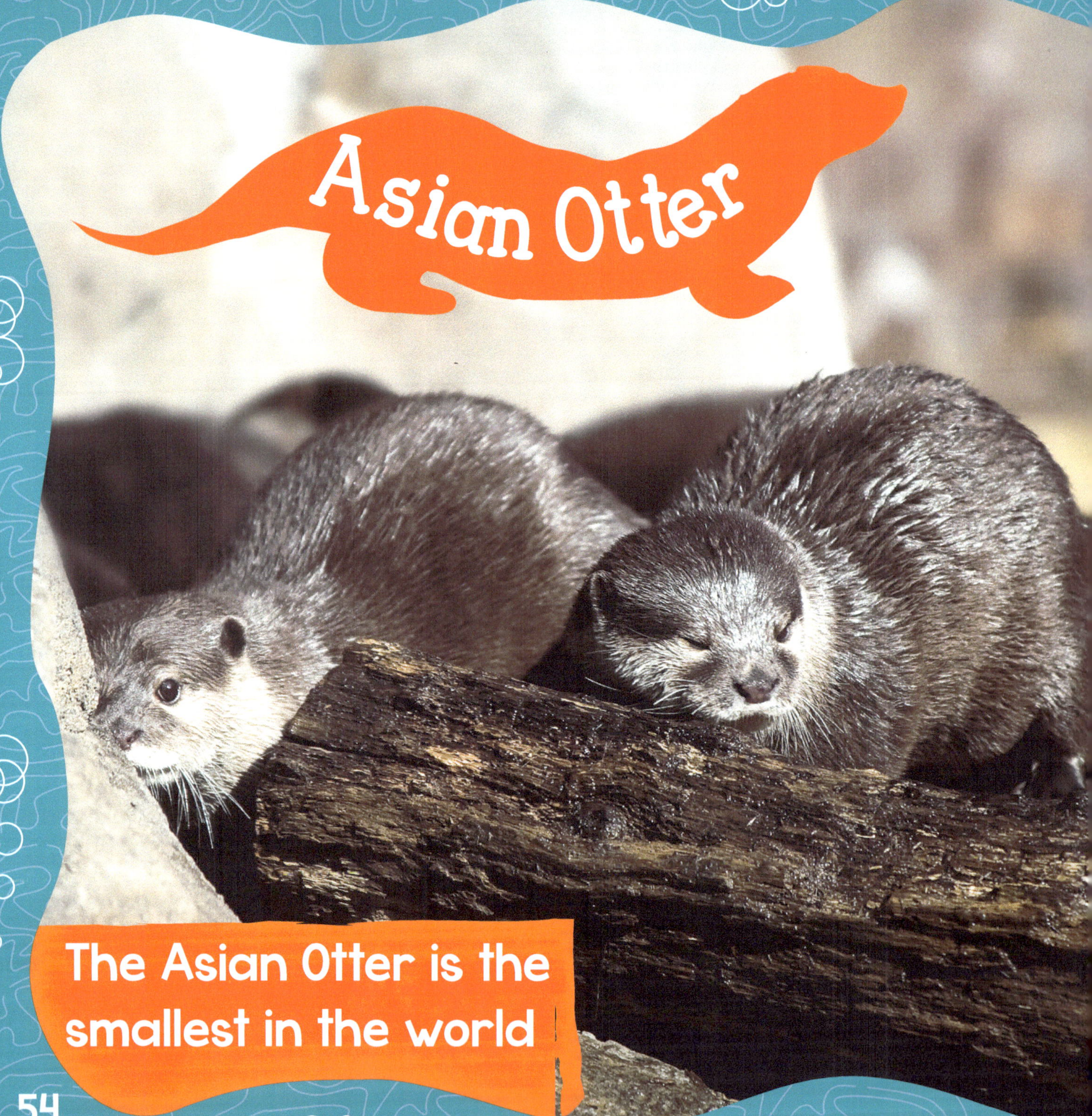

The Asian Otter is the smallest in the world

Penguin

Penguins don't jump. They bounce!

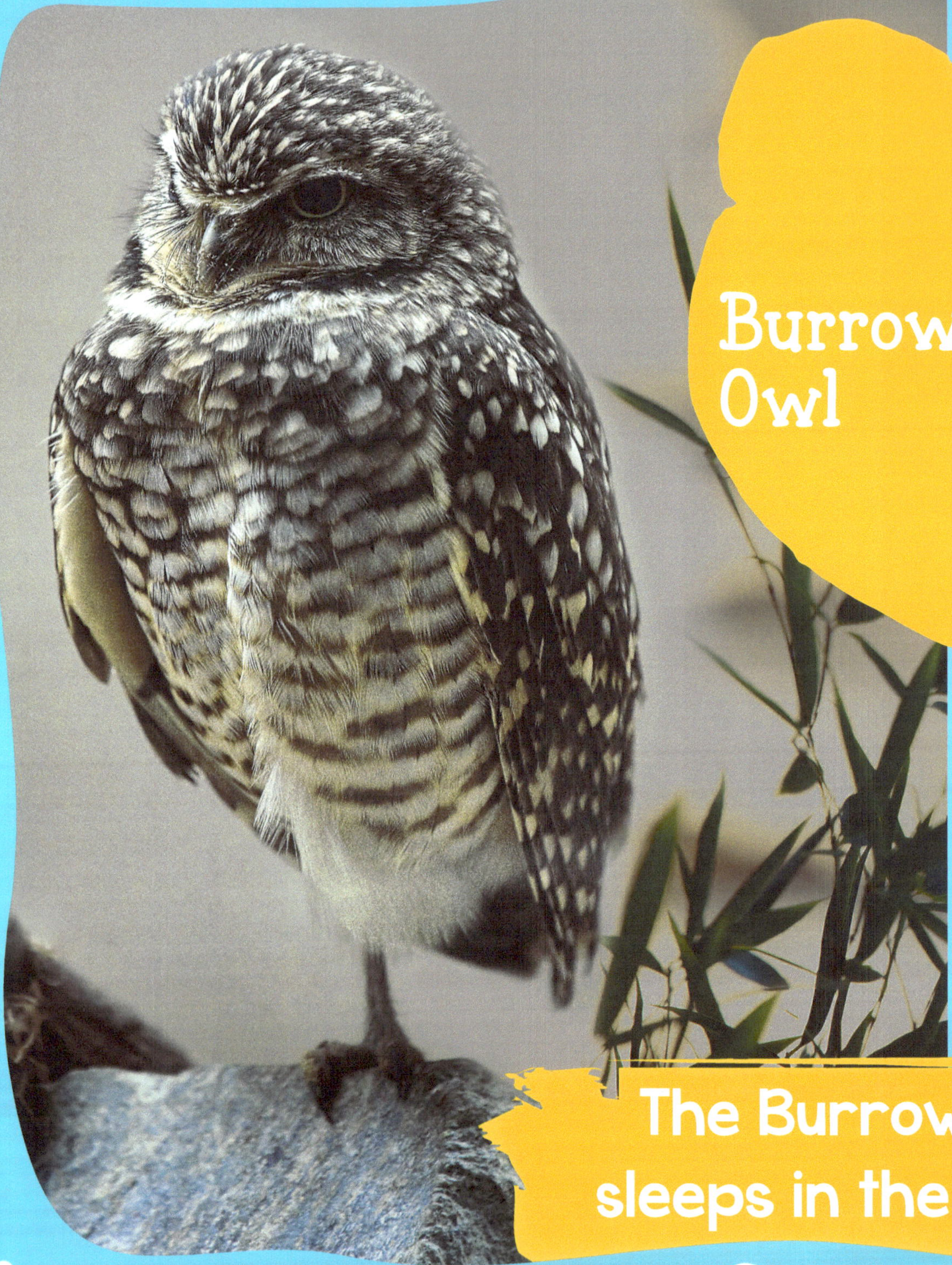

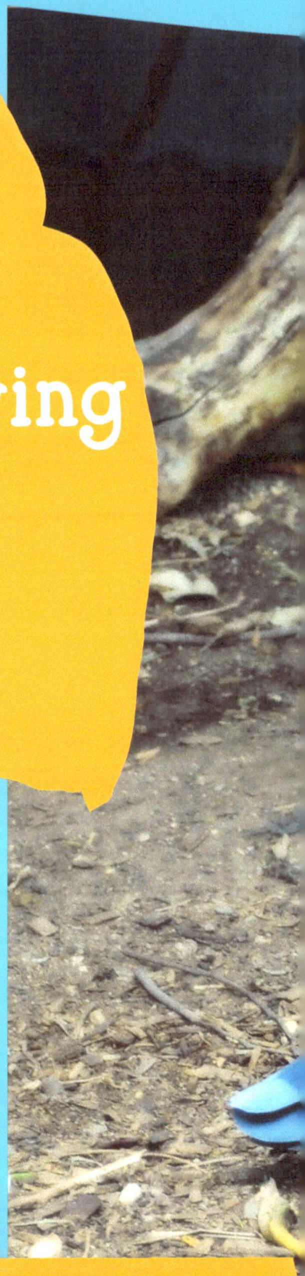

Burrowing Owl

The Burrowing Owl sleeps in the ground

Goura-crowned Pigeon

Goura Pigeons are the largest in the world

57

Seagull

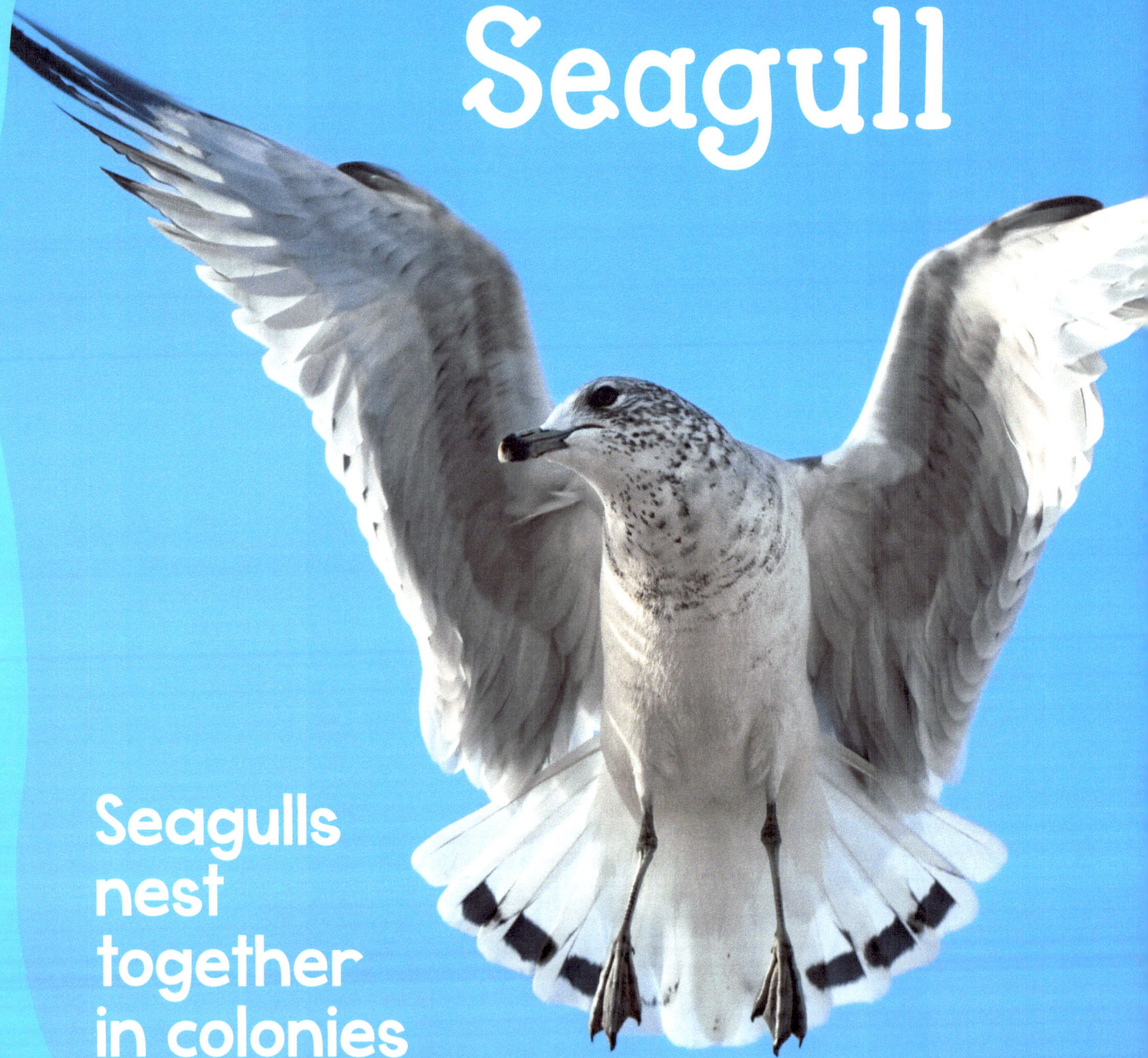

Seagulls
nest
together
in colonies

Pelican

Pelicans catch fish in their bills

Giant Panda

Giant Pandas like to be alone

Giant Pandas eat bamboo

Red Panda

The Red Panda
eats bamboo

The Red Panda
is sometimes
called a fire cat

Przhevalsky's Horse

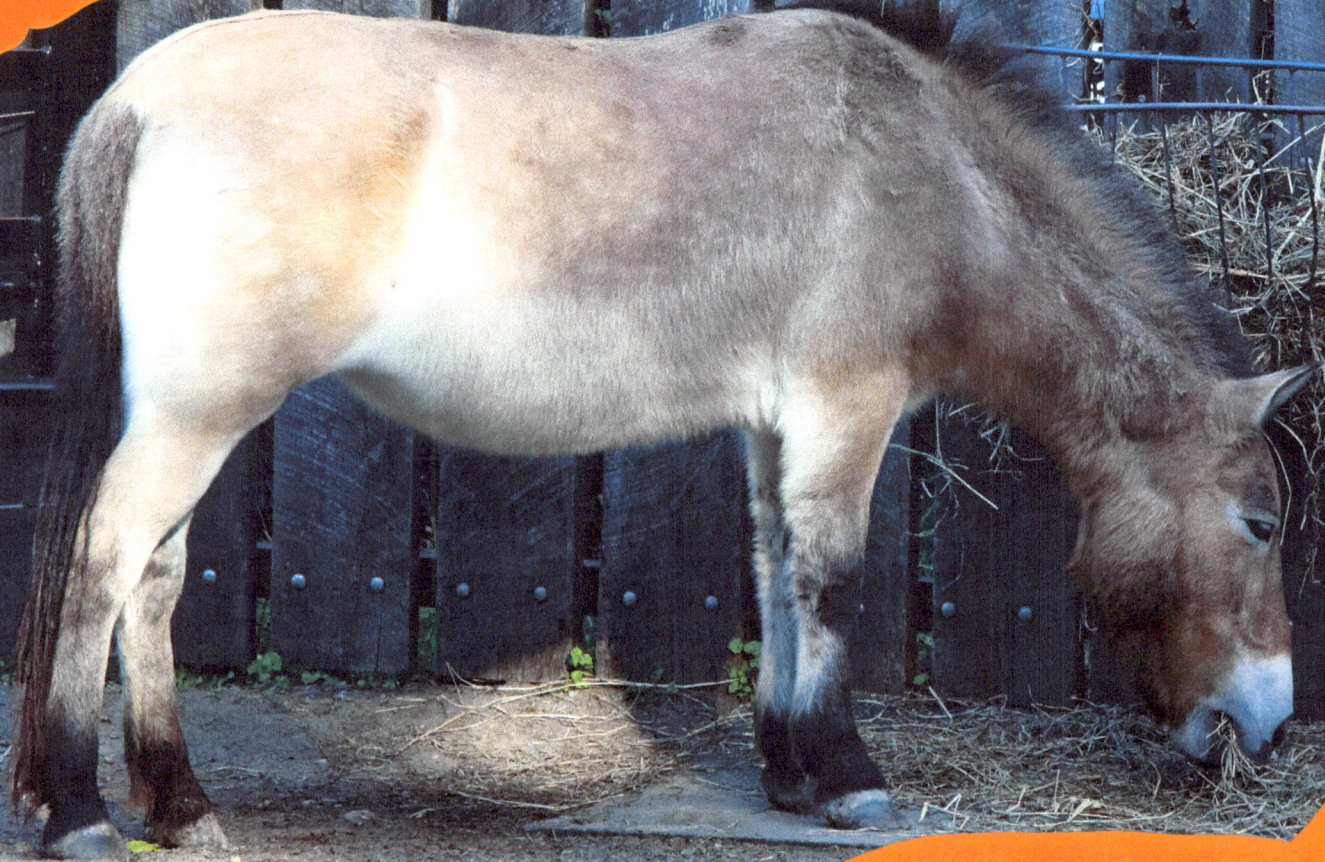

This horse is from Mongolia

Kangaroo

A baby Kangaroo is called joey

Polar Bear

Polar Bears live near the North Pole

Polar Bears don't hibernate

Polar Bears like to catch fish

65

Keel-billed Toucan

The Toucan's bill is like a saw

Parrots

Some Parrots can talk like humans

Greater Rhea

The Greater Rhea can't fly

Pink Flamingo

Flamingos even sleep standing on one leg

Red-legged Seriema

The Seriema Bird lives in South America

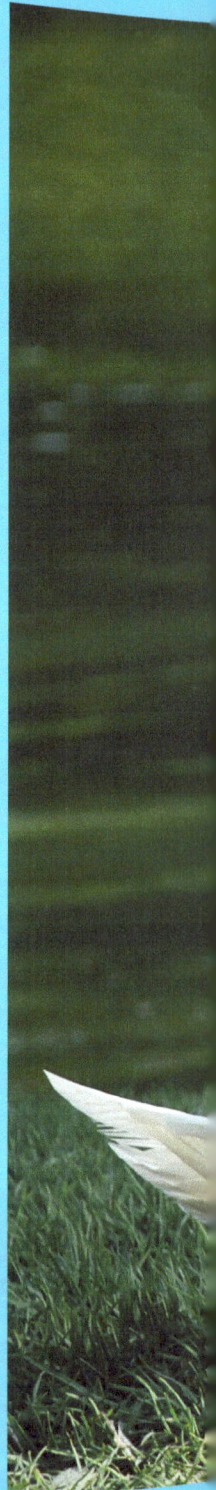

Swan

A Baby Swan is called a cygnet

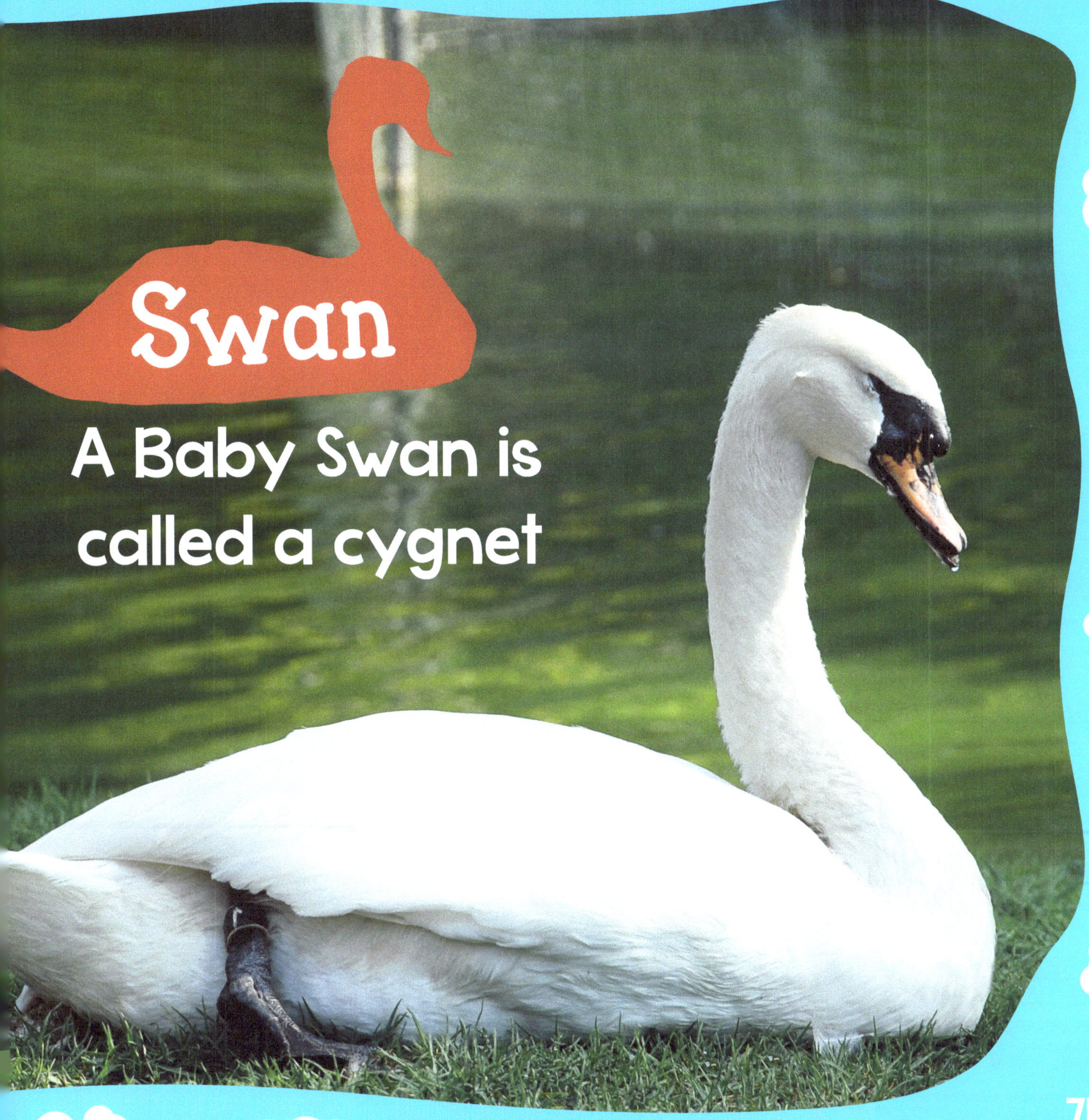

Seal

Male Seals are called bulls

Baby Seals are called pups

Seals can swim underwater for a very long time

Orange Knee Tarantula

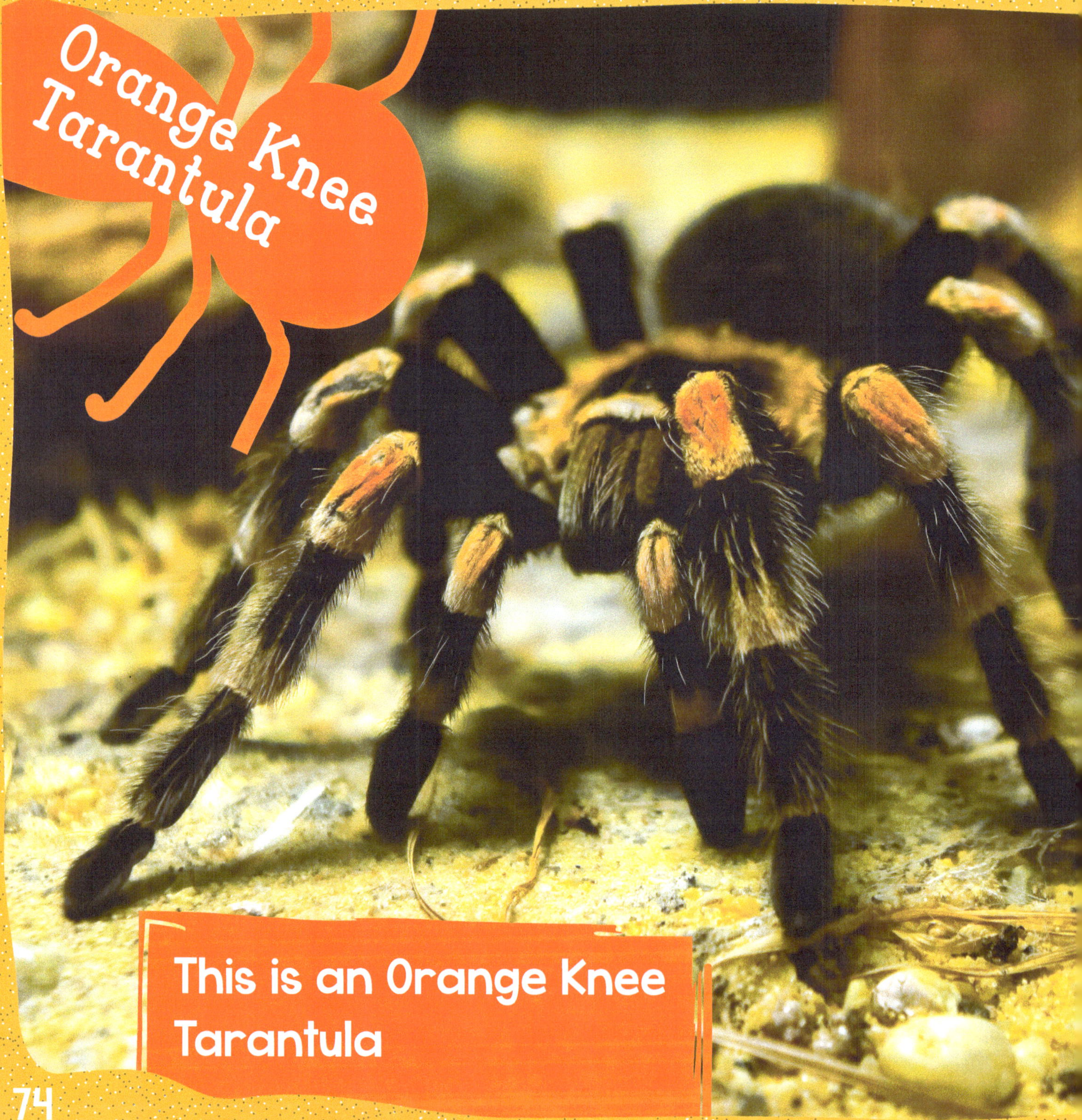

This is an Orange Knee Tarantula

Goliath Bird-eating Tarantula

Tarantulas can be as big as dinner plates

White Bengal Tiger

The Tiger is the largest of the big cats

Sumatran Tiger

Tiger babies are called cubs

Tortoise

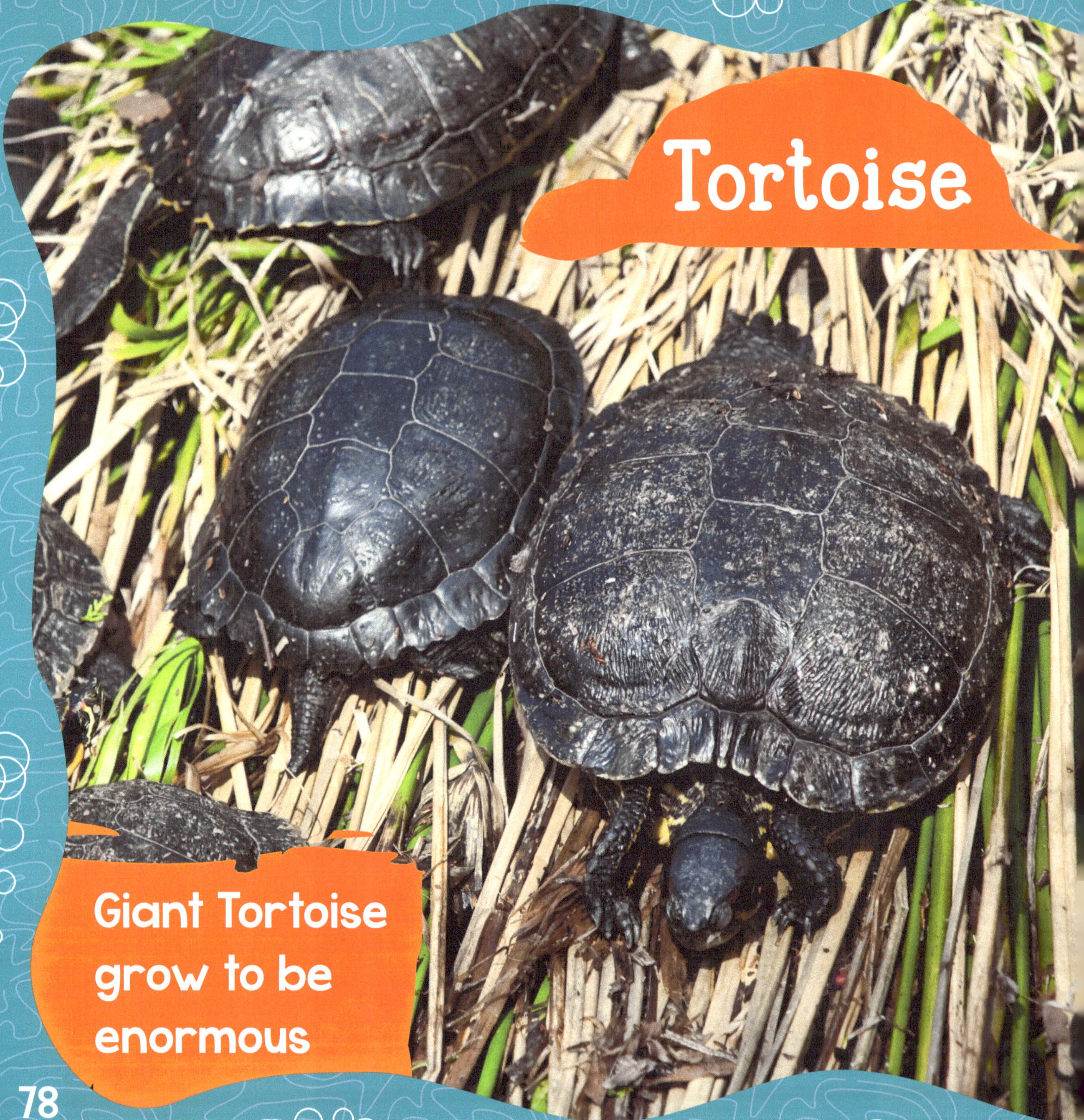

Giant Tortoise grow to be enormous

Giant Tortoise

Some Giant Tortoise live for over 100 years

Warthog

Warthogs live in groups called sounders

Suidae Wild Pig

The Suidae Wild Pig's cousin is the farm pig

Suidae Wild Pigs are very smart

Zebra

Zebras mostly eat grass

Zebras live in herds

Zebras stand up while they sleep

www.ingramcontent.com/pod-product-compliance
Lightning Source LLC
Chambersburg PA
CBHW061046090426
42740CB00002B/61